Let a special kid in your life know you care—stash a note from *Notes to Share* in their lunchbox, backpack, or sports bag! Within this little book, there are six types of notes:

- Inspirational quotes that will have little Rebels dreaming big
- Pick-me-ups sure to add some sweetness to even the sourest of days
- Personalizable messages to keep parents and kids feeling connected
- Fun facts perfect for sharing at lunch tables
- Jokes that will have the whole family giggling

Notes to Share show you care!

Good Night Stories for Rebel Girls and Rebel Girls are registered trademarks.

Good Night Stories for Rebel Girls and all other Rebel Girls titles are available for bulk purchase for sale promotions, premiums, fundraising, and educational needs. For details, write to sales@rebelgirls.com.

Rebel Girls, Inc.
421 Elm Ave.
Larkspur, CA 94939
www.rebelgirls.com

Author: Molly Reisner
Art director: Giulia Flamini
Graphic designer: Kristen Brittain
Editors: Jess Harriton
Special thanks: Eliza Kirby, Grace Srinivasiah, Sarah Parvis

Printed in China
First Edition: May 2023
10 9 8 7 6 5 4 3 2 1
ISBN: 978-1-953424-48-8

FSC
www.fsc.org
MIX
Paper | Supporting
responsible forestry
FSC™ C018179

NOTES to SHARE

"I want to still have a sharp pen and a thin skin and an open heart."

—Taylor Swift, singer-songwriter

Illustration by Anna Dixon

FUN FACT

By the time she was seven years old, architect Zaha Hadid was already designing. She designed her own childhood bedroom!

REBEL GIRLS

Illustration by Noa Snir

No matter what day or year, one thing's always true: your smile is contagious.
I love the joy in you!

WHEN YOU GET HOME, LET'S

_____ !

What did bird scientist Mya-Rose Craig say to the chicks before they went to sleep?

Tweet dreams!

Illustration by Julia Kuo

"If everything was perfect, you would never learn and you would never grow."

—Beyoncé, singer, songwriter, and businesswoman

Illustration by Eline Van Dam

Amelia Earhart was the first woman to fly nonstop and solo across the Atlantic Ocean. She always had an adventurous spirit. As a kid, she built her own backyard roller coaster!

Illustration by Giulia Flamini

My wish for you
today is that

_____

_____

Why did reptile expert Joan Beauchamp Procter give her lizard piano lessons?

So he could practice playing his scales.

Illustration by Marijke Buurlage

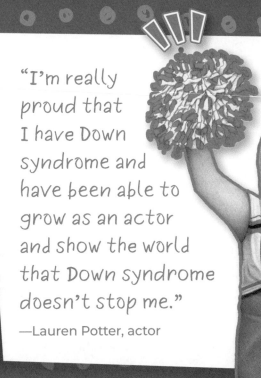

"I'm really proud that I have Down syndrome and have been able to grow as an actor and show the world that Down syndrome doesn't stop me."

—Lauren Potter, actor

Illustration by Alice Barberini

FUN FACT

February 22 is officially recognized as Rihanna Day in her home country of Barbados. But jamming out to her music is fun on any day!

Illustration by Jestenia Southerland

Feeling anxious?
Try this:

1. Name three things you see.

2. Name three sounds you hear.

3. Move three parts of your body.

Now let that stress ball float up to the stratosphere!

WHAT IS PHOTOGRAPHER VIVIAN MAIER'S FAVORITE PART OF A STORM?

WHEN THERE'S A BIG FLASH OF LIGHTNING!

Illustration by Sara Olmos

"I'm not going to continue knocking that old door that doesn't open for me. I'm going to create my own door and walk through that."

—Ava DuVernay, filmmaker

Illustration by Adesewa Adekoya

Best-selling writer Agatha Christie is known for her marvelous mysteries, but she also wrote romance novels under a pen name: Mary Westmacott.

What would your pen name be?

Illustration by Giulia Tomai

YOU'RE A RAY OF

Smart

Understanding

Nifty

Silly

Honorable

Interesting

Nice

Excellent

You made me crack
up that time you

_____

_____

_____ !

WHY DOES ZOOLOGIST LUCY KING TRAVEL WITH AN ELEPHANT?

For the extra trunk space.

Illustration by Jennifer M. Potter

Illustration by Eline Van Dam

Speedy Italian cyclist Alfonsina Strada won her first bike race in 1904, when she was 13. Her prize? A pig!

FUN FACT

Illustration by Cristina Portolano

IT'S COOL
2 B KIND

A few reasons why
you're the best!

1. _____

2. _____

3. _____

What is tennis star Serena Williams's favorite veggie?

Muscle sprouts!

Illustration by Camilla Ru

"I have learned you are never too small to make a difference."

—Greta Thunberg, climate activist

Illustration by Paula Zamudio

FUN FACT

The first female filmmaker, Alice Guy Blaché, made a one-minute film called "The Cabbage Fairy" in 1896, which was one of the first films to tell a made-up story!

Illustration by Helen Li

What made you LOL today?

Write it on the back so you won't forget.
(And tell me later. I want to LOL too!)

What is gymnast Suni Lee's favorite cold treat?

An ice-cream twist!

Illustration by Danielle Elysse

Illustration by Marta Signori

NOT ONLY IS OLYMPIC GOLD WINNER ALLYSON FELIX A LIGHTNING-FAST RUNNER, SHE'S ALSO A PASSIONATE HULA-HOOPER!

FUN FACT

Illustration by Kim Holt

Off the top of my head, three adjectives that remind me of you:

#1: _____

#2: _____

#3: _____

What name did marine biologist Sylvia Earle give to an eight-tentacled sea creature who always knows the time?

A clock-topus!

Illustration by Geraldine Sy

Illustration by Sarah Madden

FUN FACT

The world can thank nurse Florence Nightingale for making sure everyone washes their hands at the hospital! She developed cleanliness standards for patient care in the 1800s.

Illustration by Dalila Rovazzani

All aboard the compliment train!

Give a compliment, then ask that person to choo-choo-choose someone else to compliment.

You surprised
me (in a good
way!) when you

_____.

Why does fashion designer Diane von Fürstenberg love salad?

Because she can choose her favorite dress-ing!

Illustration by Elisa Seitzinger

"Nothing is impossible. The word itself says 'I'm possible!'"

—Audrey Hepburn, actor and humanitarian

Illustration by Marta Signori

FUN FACT

During World War II, Paris-based entertainer Josephine Baker was a spy for the French Resistance. She pinned top-secret info to her undergarments and wrote messages in invisible ink on her sheet music.

Illustration by Tyla Mason

Feelings Check-In!
Circle two moods.
Let's chat about
them later!

Silly
Sleepy
Bored
Curious
Annoyed
Relaxed
Nervous
Sad
Excited
Happy
Confused
Focused
Positive

YOU REALLY LET YOUR THOUGHTFULNESS SHINE THROUGH WHEN

_____ .

HOW DOES ROCK AND ROLLER JOAN JETT DECORATE HER HOUSE FOR HALLOWEEN?

WITH LOTS OF PUNK-INS!

Illustration by Annalisa Ventura

"You can't use up creativity. The more you use, the more you have."

—Maya Angelou, author

Illustration by Thandiwe Tshabalala

Teenage inventor alert! At 16, Ann Makosinski invented a flashlight that's powered by . . .

A. the sun
B. body heat from someone's hand
C. fire
D. all of the above

FUN FACT

Answer: The correct answer is C, because that's what you hold the flashlight with!

Illustration by Claudia Carieri

You're a

Resilient
Awesome
Inclusive
Neat
Beautiful
Outstanding
Wonderful

Just a short list of
people who love you!

REBEL GIRLS

What dish did chef Julia Child make for her mother?

A mom-elette.

Illustration by Barbara Dziadosz

"Like art, revolutions come from combining what exists into what has never existed before."

—Gloria Steinhem, journalist and political activist

Illustration by Malin Rosenqvist

ON JULY 30, 2002,
BASKETBALL PLAYER
LISA LESLIE MADE
HISTORY
WHEN SHE
BECAME
THE FIRST
PLAYER
TO DUNK
IN THE WNBA.

REBEL GIRLS

SPARKS
9

FUN FACT

Illustration by Kim Holt

A little note to say
I love you lots.

Remember when you
overcame your fear of

_____

by _____ ?

Yeah, that was pretty cool!

What is Queen Elizabeth I's favorite way to measure?

With a ruler!

Illustration by Ana Galvañ

REBEL GIRLS

"Feet, what do I need them for if I have wings to fly?"

—Frida Kahlo, painter

Illustration by Helena Morais Soares

FUN FACT

Malala Yousafzai spoke up about educational rights for Pakistani girls. To honor her courage, NASA named an asteroid after her. She is truly out of this world!

Illustration by Sara Bondi

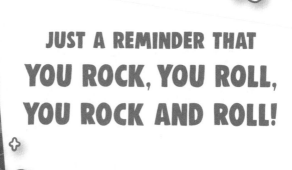

JUST A REMINDER THAT
YOU ROCK, YOU ROLL,
YOU ROCK AND ROLL!

FILL IN THIS NOTE AND PASS IT ALONG!

DEAR_____,

HI! A LITTLE NOTE TO SAY THAT I THINK

YOU'RE _____ AND HOPE YOU

HAVE A(N)_____ DAY!

SINCERELY,

_____

Illustration by Gaia Stella

"I just try to approach every opportunity on stage as if it's my first time and my last time."

—Misty Copeland, ballerina

Illustration by Ping Zhu

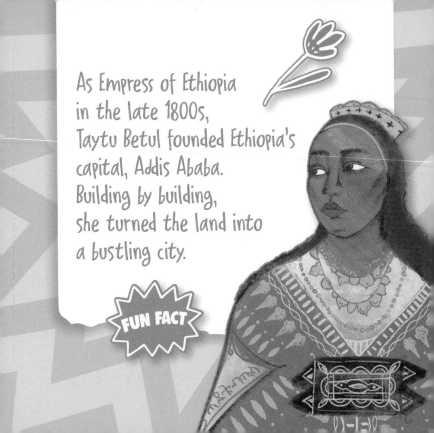

As Empress of Ethiopia in the late 1800s, Taytu Betul founded Ethiopia's capital, Addis Ababa. Building by building, she turned the land into a bustling city.

FUN FACT

Illustration by Gabrielle Tesfaye

If your day is kind of blah, close your eyes and think of a good memory. What do you see, hear, smell?

Capture that feeling and hold it in your 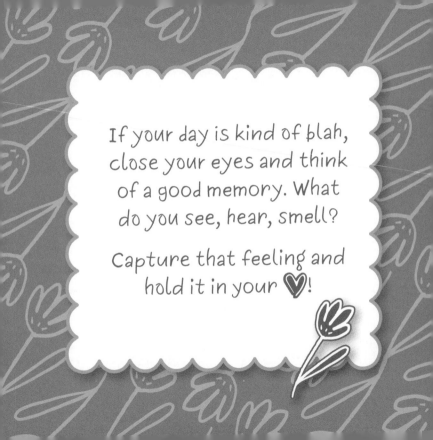!

Write down three things you want to do this month, and we'll try to make them happen!

#1:

#2:

#3:

What is ski mountaineer Kit DesLauriers' favorite direction?

Downhill!

Illustration by Xuan Loc Xuan

"Sometimes, what you're looking for is already there."

—Aretha Franklin, singer

Illustration by Johnalynn Holland

FUN FACT

Salsa singing legend Celia Cruz had a unique rallying cry when she performed: Azúcar! (Sugar!) She was honored on a US Postal Service stamp in 2011, along with fellow Rebel Girl Carmen Miranda.

Illustration by Ping Zhu

I BELIEVE
IN YOU A
BAJILLION
PERCENT.

I CAN'T WAIT TO

_____

_____

WITH YOU THIS
WEEKEND!

How does singer Gloria Estefan compose music?

She uses a notepad.

Illustration by Nan Lawson

"Only when our clever brain and our human heart work together in harmony can we achieve our full potential."

—Jane Goodall, primatologist

Illustration by Emmanuelle Walker

Legend has it, long ago, an Irish girl named Gráinne Ní Mháille, or Grace O'Malley, dressed as a boy and snuck onto a pirate ship for an expedition. Determined to lead, Grace soon became a pirate queen in charge of her own crew!

Illustration by Kathrin Honesta

Need a little calm break?
Here's a trick:

1. Breathe in for four seconds.
2. Hold for four seconds.
3. Breathe out for four seconds.
4. Repeat as you wish!

Hey you,

Guess what I'm thinking?

~~One day after school~~

this week, let's

_____

_____

xoxo,

_____

WHY IS DRUMMER NANDI BUSHELL'S SENSE OF RHYTHM SO IMPORTANT?

She counts on it!

Illustration by Sharee Miller

"If they don't give you a seat at the table, bring a folding chair."

—Shirley Chisholm, politician

Illustration by Olivia Fields

Did you know Helen Keller is featured on the Alabama quarter? Her name is also shown in Braille—a writing system using raised dots on paper for those who can't see. You could say Helen Keller really "coined" the quarter!

FUN FACT

REBEL GIRLS

Illustration by Monica Garwood

What are three things that
made you happy today?

#1: _____
_____
#2: _____
_____
#3: _____
_____

What is environmental activist Amelia Telford's least favorite insect?

A litterbug.

REBEL GiRLS

Illustration by Angela Acevedo Perez

Illustration by Nicole Miles

When she was 17, wildlife conservationist Bindi Irwin waltzed her way to win *Dancing with the Stars*! She donated her prize money to organizations that help animals.

FUN FACT

Illustration by Annalisa Ventura

WHAT SONG CAN'T YOU GET OUT OF YOUR HEAD?

_____

"You'll never do a whole lot unless you're brave enough to try."

—Dolly Parton, singer, songwriter, and philanthropist

Illustration by Janie Secker

"Everything great that ever happened in this world happened first in somebody's imagination."

—Astrid Lindgren, author

Illustration by Justine Lecouffe

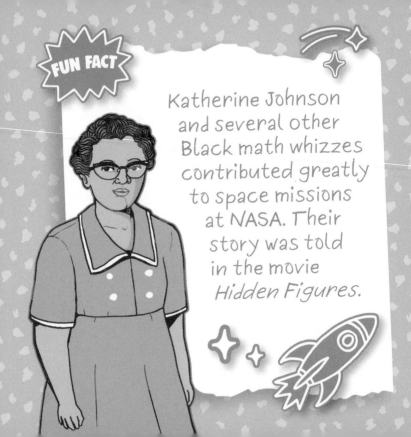

FUN FACT

Katherine Johnson and several other Black math whizzes contributed greatly to space missions at NASA. Their story was told in the movie *Hidden Figures*.

Illustration by Cristina Portolano

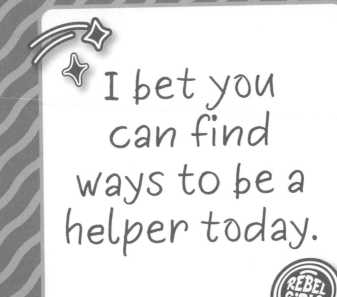

I bet you can find ways to be a helper today.

If today was a movie,
what would the title be?

_____

WHAT MUSIC DOES OLYMPIC GYMNAST ALY RAISMAN LIKE TO ROCK OUT TO?

HEAVY MEDAL

REBEL GIRLS

Illustration by Salini Perera

"Never be afraid to be a poppy in a field of daffodils."

—Michaela DePrince, ballerina

Illustration by Debora Guidi

To protect herself from the sun in the deserts of New Mexico, painter Georgia O'Keeffe would paint nature from inside her car.

Illustration by Ana Juan

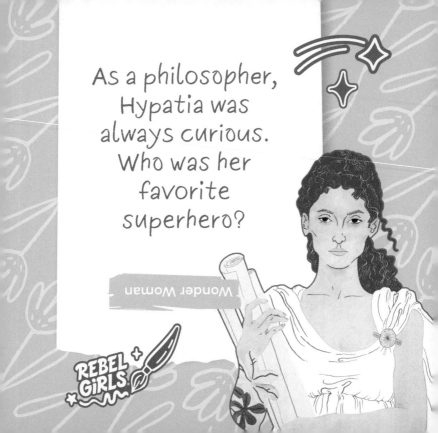

As a philosopher, Hypatia was always curious. Who was her favorite superhero?

Wonder Woman

REBEL GIRLS

Illustration by Riikka Sormunen

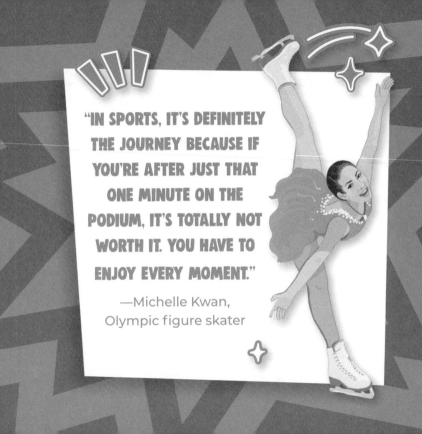

"IN SPORTS, IT'S DEFINITELY THE JOURNEY BECAUSE IF YOU'RE AFTER JUST THAT ONE MINUTE ON THE PODIUM, IT'S TOTALLY NOT WORTH IT. YOU HAVE TO ENJOY EVERY MOMENT."

—Michelle Kwan,
Olympic figure skater

Illustration by Lily Kim Qian

Fizzy Fact: Actor and inventor Hedy Lamarr created a cube that instantly carbonated water!

FUN FACT

Illustration by Marta Signori

You're a
good friend
to others.

Make a quick doodle
(and show me later)!

The Doodle Zone

Why did astronaut Samantha Cristoforetti have trouble floating in space?

She drank too much gravi-tea.

Illustration by Giulia Tomai

"DON'T TRY SO HARD TO FIT IN, AND CERTAINLY DON'T TRY SO HARD TO BE DIFFERENT . . . JUST TRY HARD TO BE YOU."

—Zendaya,
actor and singer

Illustration by Tyler Mishá Barnett

FUN FACT

In 1933, politician Eleanor Roosevelt enjoyed a plane ride from Washington, DC to Baltimore, Maryland— with Amelia Earhart!

Illustration by Lizzy Stewart

REBEL GiRLS

You've got so
many interesting
things to say.

LET'S GOALSHARE! HERE ARE THREE OF MY GOALS TODAY:

1. _____

2. _____

3. _____

WHAT ARE THREE OF YOURS?

1. _____

2. _____

3. _____

WHAT DOES FARMER WINONA LADUKE EAT WHEN SHE NEEDS A QUICK SNACK?

Corn on the job.

Illustration by Débora Islas

"Let your passion be your compass to achieving the impossible."

—Simone Manuel, Olympic swimmer

REBEL GIRLS

Illustration by Danielle Elyse Mann

FUN FACT

Cleopatra, a highly educated Egyptian pharaoh, was also a fashion and beauty trendsetter. Other women copied her unique hairstyle and pearl jewelry.

Illustration by Kiki Ljung

If you admire something someone did, let 'em know.

If today was
a flavor, how
would it taste?

Flavor of the Day:

_____

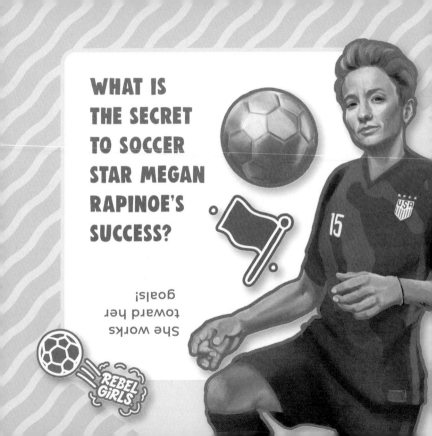

WHAT IS THE SECRET TO SOCCER STAR MEGAN RAPINOE'S SUCCESS?

She works toward her goals!

REBEL GiRLS

Illustration by Kim Holt

"One of the greatest gifts you can give is your undivided attention."

—Oprah Winfrey, TV host, producer, actor, and author

Illustration by Palesa Monareng

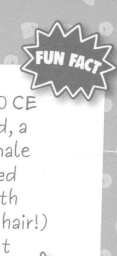

FUN FACT

Around 60 CE in England, a fierce female warrior named Boudicca (with rocking red hair!) led the fight against the invading Roman army.

REBEL GIRLS

Illustration by Monica Garwood

Write me a three-sentence story!

Once upon a time _____

_____

Suddenly, _____

_____

Fortunately, _____

_____

THE END

What is movie star Keke Palmer's favorite shape?

an act-agon!

Illustration by Noa Denmon

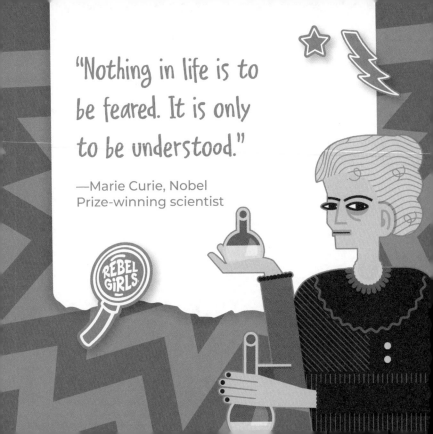

"Nothing in life is to be feared. It is only to be understood."

—Marie Curie, Nobel Prize-winning scientist

Illustration by Claudia Carieri

FUN FACT

Musical legend Julie Andrews (the OG Mary Poppins!) co-writes children's books with her daughter Emma. They've written more than 30 books together!

REBEL GiRLS.

Illustration by Jennifer M. Potter

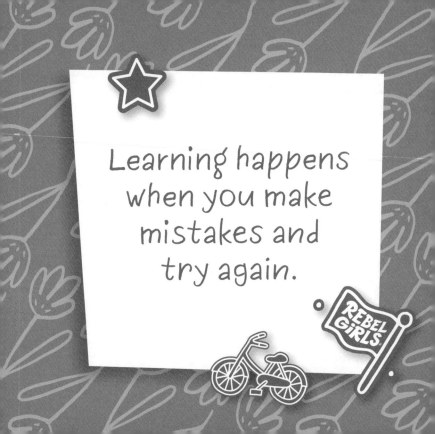

On a scale of blah to brilliant, how's your day going?

Blah   Not the worst   So-so   A-OK   Brilliant

HOW DID SPY NOOR INAYAT KHAN LIKE TO SLEEP?

Under covers.

Illustration by Yevheniia Haidamaka

"Stand for something or you will fall for anything. Today's mighty oak is yesterday's nut that held its ground."

—Rosa Parks, civil rights activist

Illustration by Sally Nixon

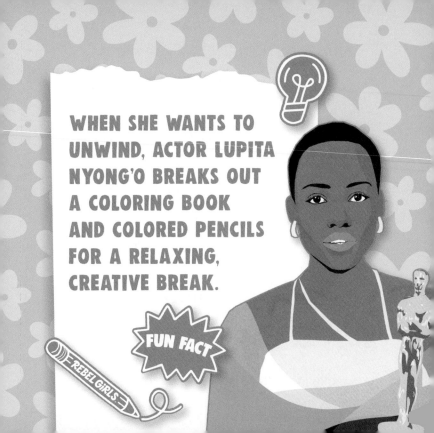

WHEN SHE WANTS TO UNWIND, ACTOR LUPITA NYONG'O BREAKS OUT A COLORING BOOK AND COLORED PENCILS FOR A RELAXING, CREATIVE BREAK.

FUN FACT

REBEL GiRLS

Illustration by Monica Ahanonu

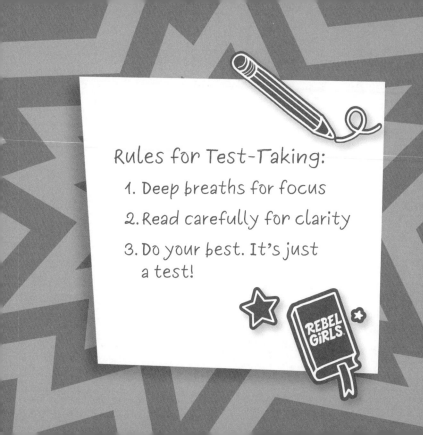

Rules for Test-Taking:

1. Deep breaths for focus

2. Read carefully for clarity

3. Do your best. It's just a test!

Feeling curious? Try to estimate how many light bulbs are in your house! Start with a guess . . .

Your Guess:

Final Lightbulb Count:

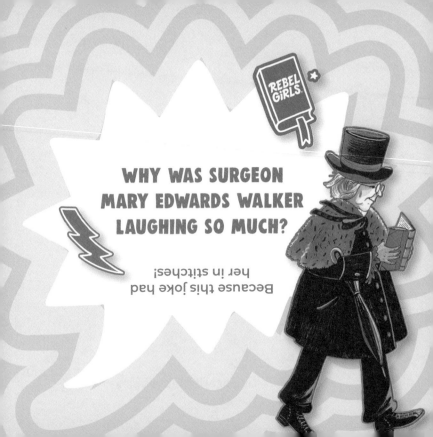

WHY WAS SURGEON
MARY EDWARDS WALKER
LAUGHING SO MUCH?

Because this joke had
her in stitches!

Illustration by Elizabeth Baddeley

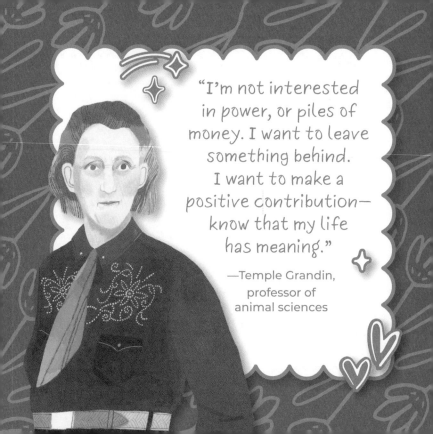

"I'm not interested in power, or piles of money. I want to leave something behind. I want to make a positive contribution—know that my life has meaning."

—Temple Grandin, professor of animal sciences

Illustration by Beatrice Cerocchi

WHEN SHE WAS 10, THEODORA VON LIECHTENSTEIN (ROYAL FACT: SHE'S A PRINCESS!) FOUNDED A CONSERVATION GROUP FOR TEENS CALLED GREEN TEEN TEAM.

FUN FACT

Illustration by Sofia Cavallari

It's OK to not know every answer.

REBEL GIRLS

WRITE DOWN THE INGREDIENTS FOR YOUR FAVORITE DISH AND LET'S MAKE IT!

RECIPE TITLE: _____

INGREDIENT LIST:

_____ _____

_____ _____

_____ _____

DID SOCCER STAR MARTA VIEIRA DA SILVA ENJOY THE PARTY?

Yes, she had a ball!

Illustration by Annalisa Ventura

"If there's a book that you want to read, but it hasn't been written yet, then you must write it."

—Toni Morrison, author

Illustration by Noa Denmon

Beatrix Potter, author of *The Tale of Peter Rabbit*, also kept a diary — written in secret code! One of her fans decoded it 20 years after she died.

FUN FACT

REBEL GIRLS

Illustration by Barbara Dziadosz

LET'S PLAN A MOVIE NIGHT!

WHAT SHOULD WE WATCH?

_____

_____

_____

REBEL GIRLS.

What
dessert did
mathematician
Ada Lovelace
enjoy?

REBEL GIRLS

Pi!

Illustration by Elisabetta Stoinich

"I STAND FOR FREEDOM OF EXPRESSION, DOING WHAT YOU BELIEVE IN, AND GOING AFTER YOUR DREAMS."

—Madonna,
singer, songwriter,
and businesswoman

Illustration by Eline Van Dam

Earning lead roles in famous ballets like *The Nutcracker*, Yuan Yuan Tan was the youngest principal dancer ever in the San Francisco Ballet—and the first from Asia.

FUN FACT

Illustration by Petra Braun

It might not always seem like it, but everything will be OK.

Let's make some
new memories and
_____ !

Why did paleontologist Mary Anning enjoy finding fossils?

She just really dug it.

Illustration by Martina Paukova

"I've been brash all my life, and it's gotten me into a lot of trouble. But at the same time, speaking out has sustained me and given meaning to my life."

—Hazel Scott, musician and activist

Illustration by Sabrena Khadija

FUN FACT

TENNIS SUPERSTAR STEFFI GRAF SERVED UP 22 GRAND SLAM WINS AND AN OLYMPIC GOLD MEDAL WITH HER POWERFUL PLAYS ON THE COURT!

Illustration by Giulia Flamini

TAKE A CHANCE—TRY A DIFFERENT APPROACH IF SOMETHING ISN'T WORKING!

ONE OF MY FAVORITE
THINGS ABOUT YOU IS

_____.

Why did investigative journalist
Nellie Bly sample every
ice cream flavor?

She wanted to get the perfect scoop!

Illustration by Zara Picken

"Because I learned long ago that winning doesn't always mean you get the prize. Sometimes you get progress, and that counts."

—Stacey Abrams, activist and politician

Illustration by Kelsee Thomas

FUN FACT

Off the slopes, snowboarder Chloe Kim races to keep up with her adorable Mini Australian Shepherd, Reese!

REBEL GIRLS

Illustration by Barbara Dziadosz

If you had a flower named after you, what kind would it be?

I'd be a _____
kind of flower because it's

_____,
_____, and
_____ like me!

YOU DON'T HAVE
TO BE MORE THAN
WHO YOU ARE.
YOU ARE ENOUGH.

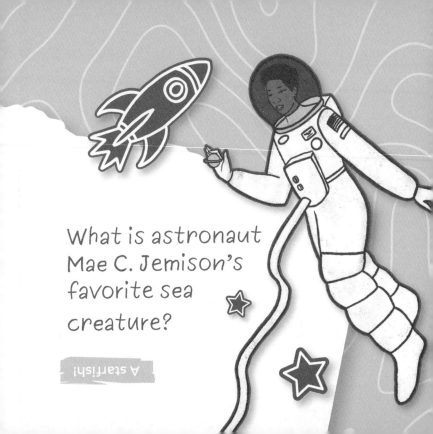

What is astronaut Mae C. Jemison's favorite sea creature?

A starfish!

Illustration by Alexandra Bowman

"I'M TRYING TO SHOW THAT YOU SHOULDN'T JUDGE SOMEONE BY HOW THEY LOOK, BECAUSE THE PERSON INSIDE CAN BE COMPLETELY DIFFERENT."

—Tegan Vincent-Cooke, para-dressage rider

Illustration by DeAndra Hodge

FUN FACT

If you're like pro skateboarder Sky Brown, then you like to start the day off sweet! Sky enjoys chocolate milk and mixing up different cereals in the AM.

Illustration by Kate Prior

The room is brighter with you in it.

What did Frankenstein, a character created by author Mary Shelley, get at the hardware store?

Fright bulbs.

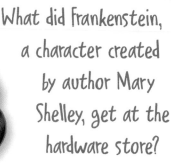

Illustration by Elisabetta Stoinich

"NOTHING'S IMPOSSIBLE AND YOU CAN MAKE THE LIFE THAT YOU WANT."

—Samarria Brevard,
Olympic skateboarder

Illustration by Sharee Miller

FUN FACT

In 2020, risk-taker Maya Gabeira broke her previous Guinness World Record for the largest wave ever surfed by a woman.
The size? 73.5 whopping feet!

REBEL GIRLS

Illustration by Martina Paukova

Happy birthday
to the _____ kid
in the world! Can't
wait to celebrate!!!

✦ What was tattoo artist Maud Stevens Wagner's childhood dream?

To make her mark on the world!

Illustration by Giulia Flamini

"My vision . . . is a world where every girl is allowed to reach her full potential, make her own choices, and live the life she chooses for herself."

—Sonita Alizadeh, rapper and activist

Illustration by Samidha Gunjal

Ever wish you could be a mermaid? Transgender TV star Jazz Jennings sure has! She even created her own line of mermaid tails when she was 12.

FUN FACT

Illustration by Amy Phelps

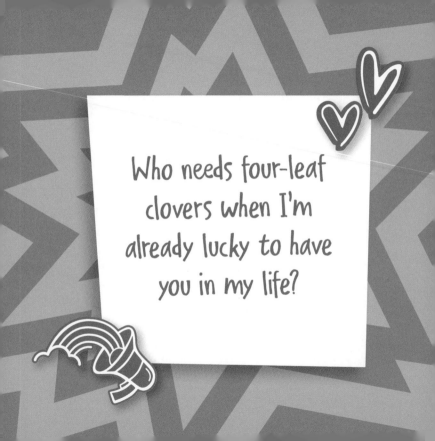

You're great at

_____!

Get out there and

_____!!

What is rapper MC Soffia's favorite snack?

Chilled beats

Illustration by Keisha Okafor

"IF IT'S A GOOD IDEA, GO AHEAD AND DO IT."

—Grace Hopper, computer scientist

Illustration by Kiki Ljung

"KIKI" WAS THE NICKNAME FOR SUPREME COURT JUSTICE RUTH BADER GINSBURG. WHEN SHE WAS A BABY, RBG KICKED A LOT!

REBEL GIRLS

FUN FACT

Illustration by Eleanor Davis

I LOVE YOUR

Honorable
Empathetic
Artistic
Radiant
Thoughtful

What is ballerina Merritt Moore's lucky number?

Two-two

Illustration by Marina Muun

"Don't mistake politeness for lack of strength."

—Sonia Sotomayor,
US Supreme Court justice

Illustration by Kathrin Honesta

To keep up with her book signings, author Margaret Atwood came up with the idea for a "remote pen." Margaret signs on an electronic pad, then wires her signature to a special drawing machine!

FUN FACT

REBEL GiRLS

Illustration by Kasia Bogdańska

Why was tennis player Naomi Osaka's party so loud?

Everyone brought a racket.

Illustration by Danielle Elysse Mann

"I'M LOUDER AND BIGGER WITH MY CURLS. THERE'S POWER IN THAT."

—Yara Shahidi,
actor and producer

REBEL GiRLS

Illustration by Natalia Agatte

FUN FACT

Motocross pro Ashley Fiolek had her own unique ride style. As a deaf biker on the racetrack, she relied on feeling engine vibrations to know when to shift gears.

Illustration by Kate Prior

HYDIL!

(HOPE YOUR DAY IS LIT!)

What is boulder climber Miho Nonaka's favorite ice cream flavor?

Rocky Road

Illustration by Salini Perera

"Be bold. If you're going to make an error, make a doozy, and don't be afraid to hit the ball."

—Billie Jean King, tennis player and activist

Illustration by Emmanuelle Walker

LMCTW!

(LET'S MAKE COOKIES THIS WEEK!)

"It's never too early to get started. It's never too early to get involved. And there's a place for you in science if you want there to be."

—Kristen Lear, conservationist and science communicator

REBEL GIRLS

Illustration by Lu Andrade

Fiona, the sick baby hippo zoo curator Chirstina Gorsuch and her team helped save, is named after Princess Fiona from the movie *Shrek*. Her ears look like an ogre's!

FUN FACT

Illustration by Izzy Evans

TRYING SOMETHING NEW IS A GREAT CONFIDENCE BOOSTER!

Life was full of adventure for trekker Barbara Hillary! When she was 75 years old, Barbara became the first Black woman to reach the North Pole.

FUN FACT

Illustration by Amari Mitnaul

Your laugh is
contagious.

ILYSM!
(I Love You So Much!)

LISTEN TO MORE EMPOWERING STORIES ON THE REBEL GIRLS APP

Download the app to listen to beloved Rebel Girls stories, as well as brand-new tales of extraordinary women. Filled with the adventures and accomplishments of women from around the world and throughout history, the Rebel Girls app is designed to entertain, inspire, and build confidence in listeners everywhere.

Scan the code to listen to unforgettable content on the Rebel Girls app!

ABOUT REBEL GIRLS

REBEL GIRLS is a global, multi-platform empowerment brand dedicated to helping raise the most inspired and confident generation of girls through content, experiences, products, and community. Originating from an international best-selling children's book, Rebel Girls amplifies stories of real-life women throughout history, geography, and field of excellence. With a growing community of nearly 20 million self-identified Rebel Girls spanning more than 100 countries, the brand engages with Generation Alpha through its book series, award-winning podcast, events, and merchandise. With the 2021 launch of the Rebel Girls app, the company has created a flagship destination for girls to explore a wondrous world filled with inspiring true stories of extraordinary women.

As a B Corp, we're part of a global community of businesses that meets high standards of social and environmental impact.

Join the Rebel Girls community:
+ Facebook: facebook.com/rebelgirls
+ Instagram: @rebelgirls
+ Twitter: @rebelgirlsbook
+ TikTok: @rebelgirlsbook
+ Web: rebelgirls.com
+ Podcast: rebelgirls.com/podcast
+ App: rebelgirls.com/app

If you liked this book, please take a moment to review it wherever you prefer!